Introduction

The world of high fashion has its own special lure. It sounds glamorous and exciting, a free ticket to luxury and fun... but what's it really like.

This book centres on the work of Betty Jackson, the award-winning designer whose clothes are admired throughout the world. You'll be able to follow the fashion process right through from the fabric, designed by the textile designer, through its selection and use by the designer, its manufacture into the fashions of next season and those garments' subsequent sale and promotion by P.R. agents and magazines.

You can read how the people who do the jobs actually see their work – its ups and downs, the hard graft it takes to get there ... and the rewards they reap.

The fashion industry is a huge employer worldwide. There are all kinds of jobs, in bewildering variety. Make no mistake – it's an industry that is heavily oversubscribed by eager hopefuls, with no easy route to success. It takes a lot of perseverance to get in, and plenty of hard work, often with long hours, to stay there.

But for many it's worth it – will you be one of them?

CONTE

TEXTILE DESIGN

Textiles are the foundation of the fashion industry. The profusion of fibres and patterns makes the clothing business what it is today, in all its complexity. The textile industry is now modern and automated – long gone is the home-spun image, replaced now by a heavy investment in technology, machinery and the latest equipment.

However, the industry in the United Kingdom is sadly in decline and generally rather behind Europe, with the possible exception of the tweed and linen mills of Scotland and Ireland. As in other areas of the fashion industry, textile designers must think internationally for employment – Italy, for instance, is the largest producer of textiles and their faith in fashion means that textile designers enjoy a very important role there. In the U.K. Courtaulds is the largest fabric group, an industrial giant which employs the majority of England-based textile specialists.

There are currently exciting developments in textiles, particularly in the influential areas of weave and knit, and these are the inspiration for many designers' work. These developments are identified by fashion forecasters who anticipate new trends in colour and fabric and report on them to their clients. The fashion year is divided into two seasons, with the beginning of the cycle marked by huge international trade fairs in London, Paris, Milan and Stuttgart. At these fairs, manufacturers exhibit their new fabric collections to designers and buyers and this is usually the starting point for most designers' work. They are backed up by lavish audio visual trend displays and presentations by trend bureaux such as Nigel French and Design Intelligence.

All the major manufacturers employ designers who work on the weave, knit, colour or print of the fabric – it has to be said, though, that about 700 textile designers graduate each year with BTEC or degree qualifications, and most never find a job in their chosen field.

Some designers set up their own studio, producing designs on paper and selling them to someone who wants to have them printed on fabric – either a fashion designer who will make them up for a collection, or a print converter who buys the designs, has them printed and then sells the fabrics to the designer. Timney-Fowler, a much-acclaimed textile design company based in London's King's Road has gone one step further, taking the design through production and manufacture right to the retail stages.

TEXTILE DESIGNER

Sue Timney is joint partner of Timney-Fowler, with husband Grahame Fowler. Sue's career began with a pre-foundation course at Çarlisle College of Art, after which she worked for four years as a photography and graphics assistant. Her foundation course and BA Honours degree in Fine Arts were at Newcastle-upon-Tyne Polytechnic and were followed by a Distinction in her post-graduate course in Textiles and Tapestry. Two years at the Royal College of Art (where she subsequently taught Textiles) brought her a Masters degree and gained her scholarships to New York and Japan.

It was in 1979 that Sue, in partnership with her husband Grahame Fowler, set up Timney-Fowler:

'We developed from a small studio, selling our designs printed on paper, to becoming our own converters, with half a dozen of our own designers. We began to control production ourselves and progressed to making up garments. We have a very definite point of view, a distinctive design statement, so it's silly for us all to sell it to someone else – we get much greater satisfaction in producing it ourselves. In addition to that, we had decided we would really like to open a retail outlet, so it was natural to see the whole process through. We began by doing our own printing, but due more to time than lack of skill, we had to hand over some of the time-consuming aspects of the processes – nowadays, we leave the very specialised areas to the experts in that field. Printing, for instance, is a very precise skill, with different fabrics taking colour in different ways – we find out the best place, the best method and the best price for the design to be printed on the particular fabric.

'Now, as well as producing, printing, making and selling our own prints (for clothes and interiors), we also do some licensing – that involves a bigger company coming along and paying for the Timney-Fowler look and name. They then do all the production for the items we've agreed on and we do the designing and get a royalty. They have a guaranteed network of sales with the capability to sell much more than we ever could.'

Sue emphasises the difficulties in finding a job in textile design:

'We employ six full-time designers here, together with a handful of students. We get about four letters a day from students, asking to come and work here, but take only a few because we prefer to employ designers full-time so that they develop with us. They have to have an excellent portfolio to stand a chance of getting into textile design. Most of the designers we take are ex-Royal College of Art students – Grahame and I both studied there and we know we will get consistent quality. It's the only purely post-graduate art college in the country. Students take a BA degree elsewhere and an MA at the Royal College. There are so many textile graduates that we can afford to take the best – it's lucky for employers but tough on the graduates.'

For Timney-Fowler to retain their distinctive look, Sue and Grahame have to keep strong control over what's being produced:

'The designers can't simply have free rein to produce what they want – it would be chaos! Once we've decided on the overall style, according to the season and the look we want to create, Grahame and I continually guide everyone – we have to be constantly on top of what's going on, although we're also continually exploring new possibilities or we would all stagnate.

'Every week each designer is given a new project to work on. We decide carefully what I'm going to give each one, bearing in mind their individual preferences and talents and discuss it with them. They'll then have a set brief to work to around that theme. They begin with a piece of paper or fabric and print, paint or mark-make onto it. If they know that the end result is a specific garment, they'll have to take that into account and consider the suitability of the design. That leads on to different shapes and colours. A designer like Betty Jackson might have a design in the back of her mind when she comes to buy from us. She might find something similar – or better – she may commission something specific from us.

'Once we've worked on the design, we have to consider colours. We make exactly the shade we want and the colourist at the printers mixes up colours to match it – an art in itself. The printer will send us samples and after a certain amount of to-ing and fro-ing, the work is approved and they go ahead and print the metreage.

'It's an exciting and stimulating job. You have to be prepared to work long hours as a textile designer (if you want a job that's 9 to 5, you're looking in the wrong direction) – but it's satisfying ... and fun!'

WAYS IN

Getting into textile design is certainly not easy! You need talent and tenacity, coupled with an excellent portfolio, but you also need technical ability. Sue Timney emphasises the importance of having experienced all aspects of the process, from design to printing. Many manufacturers complain that technical proficiency is undervalued at college – graduates may be good designers, but if they can't apply their work in a commercial world, they're of little use to employers.

Make sure that the course or combination of courses that you follow gives you practical know-how. Check that the college you wish to apply to has links with the textile industry (what placements can they arrange for you?) and consider adding another string to your bow by including a non-design option which will increase your flexibility on graduation.

You can study textile design at BTEC/SCOTVEC National Certificate/Diploma level (entry – minimum of three-four GCSE/SCE S grades), Higher National Certificate/Diploma level or degree level.

BTEC/SCOTVEC courses last for two years full-time or two/three years part-time. Degree courses can be four-year sandwich courses with industrial placements or three or four-year courses which may or may not include some work experience. BTEC/SCOTVEC and BSc courses and sandwich courses are more industry-orientated than BA courses – read prospectuses carefully.

Very few students study for a degree/HND straight after A levels/H grades – the preferred entry is via a foundation course in art and design. That will give you the chance to work in different design disciplines before having to make a final choice. Most colleges prefer applicants to have two A levels/H grades (art A level is preferred; GCSE/SCE S grade art is essential). Selection for a place involves an interview and presentation of a portfolio of work.

FASHION DESIGN

Fashion design covers a wealth of areas – designers may specialise in footwear or hats, lingerie or gloves ... but the majority design clothes.

Clothing design falls into three main sectors – couture, designer ready-to-wear and wholesale manufacture (the largest employer).

In COUTURE, clothes are designed and made for individual clients, perhaps only several hundred customers in the world being able to afford the thousands of pounds which a couture garment will cost them – a couture suit can have up to 200 hours of work in it, and will look as good inside out. Couture may be used as a loss-making flagship to promote a house style or perfume, for example (such as Dior or Chanel) and it's also an experimental breeding ground for new ideas. Couture is dominated by designer 'names', so the most likely prospect of employment for a new designer is as a designer's assistant. It's an education in itself, with less likelihood of designing any clothes but a lot of running around, co-ordinating production, liaising with the press and chasing up fabric orders. It could also mean being in charge of a studio of designers, forming the link between them and the 'name'.

DESIGNER READY-TO-WEAR is arguably the most influential area of fashion. International buyers view twice yearly collections at shows in March and October, which are extensively featured in the press. Clothes may be sold under a designer's own-name range, like Jasper Conran or Helen Storey; or under a company name such as Escada or MaxMara (the biggest area of employment for designers). Designers in this field work in design studios, either for a particular company, such as Warehouse, or for a trend bureau like Design Intelligence. They're far more likely to have a creative role, similar to the designers who work for Timney-Fowler's textile business. Some designers go on to become self-employed design consultants, based at home but travelling to see clients in France, Germany or Italy. It's very much an international business, with British designers sought after abroad because of the high standard of British art and design education. Most designers will work overseas for some time in their career.

Designer ready-to-wear and companies' less expensive 'diffusion' lines will be made in greater quantity than couture, but not as great as WHOLESALE MANUFACTURE, the sector which supplies the high street stores with the clothes you see every day.

FASHION DESIGNER

Betty Jackson is one of Britain's leading **designers,** who has built up an international reputation and sells all over the world. Fashion, though, wasn't Betty's first choice of career:

'I was supposed to be going to university to ready history and English, but at the last minute I got cold feet and announced to my headmistress that I was going to art school instead! The foundation course covered every discipline imaginable. Sculpture particularly appealed to me, but I found I was allergic to plaster of Paris, which seemed to present a major obstacle at the time! Consequently, I went to Birmingham College of Art to do a degree in Fashion and Textiles.

'Whatever you do before you embark on a career as a designer, it's important to have a basic combination of knowledge of fabrics (how they react together, what will happen to a fabric when you cut it, what sort of structure it will make); and familiarity with practical skills (how to construct a garment, from start to finish). It's simply not enough to be able to sit and draw dresses! You need to be able to explain to the people who are skilled at pattern cutting or making up exactly what you are aiming for. That technical side can be a very tedious part of a student's course, but it's one that, like piano practice, if you persevere it will pay dividends in the end.

'After I graduated I became a freelance fashion illustrator for a while, simply because I had a very bad car accident which meant that I couldn't move around – and illustrating is something that you can do sitting in one place. I knew I wanted to work as a designer in this country – it was just a question of making the right contacts. I met someone who had recently started up a company on her own, designing, making and selling clothes. We liked each other immediately and it seemed a good idea to pool our resources.

'It was great fun. We produced a small collection each season, made up samples, went and sold from them and then rushed home to get our outworkers to make them up! I was soon offered a job at Quorum, a large, well-known organisation run by Ossie Clark, a famous designer of the '70s. I joined them as a freelance designer, having negotiated my own name on the label (i.e. *Betty Jackson at Quorum*) and keeping my independence to carry on with freelance illustration. I had my own studio there and, with a cutter and a machinist, produced a range of clothes. It was only then that I realised how very tightly structured a business had to be if it were to be successful.'

Betty stayed there for six years, designing for all three labels under the Quorum umbrella – Quorum (elite and expensive), Coopers (young, trendy street fashion) and Radley (high street 'mass market' fashion). It was an experience which highlighted the vast extremes within the fashion industry. At one moment Betty would be designing something for Quorum, with no expense spared – the next she might be trying to get the cost of a shirt down for Radley so that it could retail at £9.99!

'It gave me a wonderful breadth of knowledge and also allowed me to travel. I went to India, Portugal and Hong Kong and made use of the time to learn all aspects of the business, including the sales side.'

In 1981 Betty set up her own business:

'I couldn't afford to employ anyone, but in order to make enough money to do so I had to get a collection out and sell it! I used the team at Quorum, who worked in their spare time to produce the 35 pieces for my first show ... all in one month! I showed at Olympia and took orders on the samples. People already knew a little about me and the collection was received very favourably. We showed the collection in October and delivered in January. In the interim time I was approached by Monsoon to do a collection for them.'

Betty then won Separates Designer of the Year. She hasn't looked back. Betty now has three collections a year and shows in London and Paris, with 270 pieces in each collection. She has a shop on London's Brompton Road and others within shops such as Harrods, Liberty's and Harvey Nichols … and she's won numerous other accolades, including British Designer of the Year. So how does the process work?

'You have to learn to let people concentrate on the areas in which they are experts – let textile designers like Sue Timney and Grahame Fowler design the fabric, let the expert pattern cutters make the patterns. I concentrate on designing clothes. I start with the fabric and the mood it conjures up, taking into account its softness or hardness, mattness or shininess. I go to Italy and France to look at fabrics and the London people come to my studio in London to show me theirs. I might work with a print designer to produce exactly what I want – or I may find what I'm looking for or better, with no problem at all.

'After I've made sketches they are discussed with the pattern cutter who knows and understands the fabric and can cut the pattern accordingly. A sample cutter cuts the pattern out in cloth and a machinist makes up the garment. From there a collection is built up and shown to buyers and the press. The buyers' orders will be made up by manufacturers … and so the process continues. Everything builds up to the show each season, with tremendous tension behind the scenes to ensure that everything is perfect. The very next day, though, I may have to be on a plane to Italy to buy the fabric for the next collection. There's no time to bask in the glory!'

Betty admits that you have to be *very* disciplined in this job. It's extremely pressurised, especially since the designer is responsible for the whole business and everyone else's job:

'It's important to keep your feet on the ground – you *have* to be able to read a balance sheet and know about cash flows, budgets and schedules of work. Everything stands or falls by you. There are moments of glamour – when you get a fabric dyed to just the right shade and cut in a special way and made up into a wonderful garment and someone looks absolutely gorgeous in it … that makes it all worthwhile!'

WAYS IN

Most designers have some formal training. In theory, it is possible to train in a designer's workroom, learning as you go along, but in practice a full-time college course is virtually essential.

You can study design through BTEC/SCOTVEC National Certificate/Diploma and Higher National Diploma courses, or a BA degree which can be taken after a one-year foundation course in art and design. A degree course involves studio work, with few formal lectures, if any. Experts working within the industry will give additional talks to students, who work on specific projects for the first two years, culminating in their final year show. That's an exciting affair involving a great deal of hard work but the reward of seeing their own collection on a catwalk. Graduates may then progress to a Master's degree at the Royal College of Art in London.

Courses may have a bias towards design or combine design with technology – there is usually some overlap. Clothing technology courses have a technical bias, with the emphasis on garment production, construction and management. When they have a design element, these courses are particularly suitable for people who want to specialise in design for wholesale manufacture. There are also courses available with specialist design options, such as footwear, knitwear or costume design.

And when you're looking for a job, clutching your portfolio, make sure that the work you're showing relates to that company's business. Show them that you can design something with their customer in mind. Designers now *have* to be able to relate to the commercial world and the needs of their customers.

Midseason 1991

ADVICE from Ian Griffiths, Head of Fashion designate at Kingston University

'Choose your college and your course with care. To succeed, fashion graduates have to combine creativity with commercial awareness and an individual style – they need a good, sound training in all aspects, including the technical side, and their course needs to be linked with industry so that they keep their feet on the ground and have a feel for what's going on.

'Here at Kingston we have tremendously strong links with the industry. We have only three full-time staff, the rest being visiting lecturers who actually work in the business. Staff themselves have strong ties with the industry – I, for instance, am a consultant to MaxMara, dividing my time between London and Milan.

'It's essential to find out what a college is like before you apply. Read prospectuses carefully, visit the college, look at the standard of work and talk to students who are there.

'Before students take their degree or HND course, they will have completed either a foundation course (with an emphasis on creativity and self-expression) or a BTEC/SCOTVEC course (either a general course or one with a more technical bias, including production, pattern cutting, merchandising and buying). Decide what you think your aims and abiliites are before you choose and consider all areas of fashion.

'Folders (portfolios) and personalities get people jobs. Make sure your folder reflects the needs of the place you're applying to. You need to have the courage of your own convictions and belief in your abilities, combined with constant self-criticism.

'No course can wave a magic wand and turn you into a success in the fashion industry. You have to have determination, motivation and, above all, a great amount of talent.'

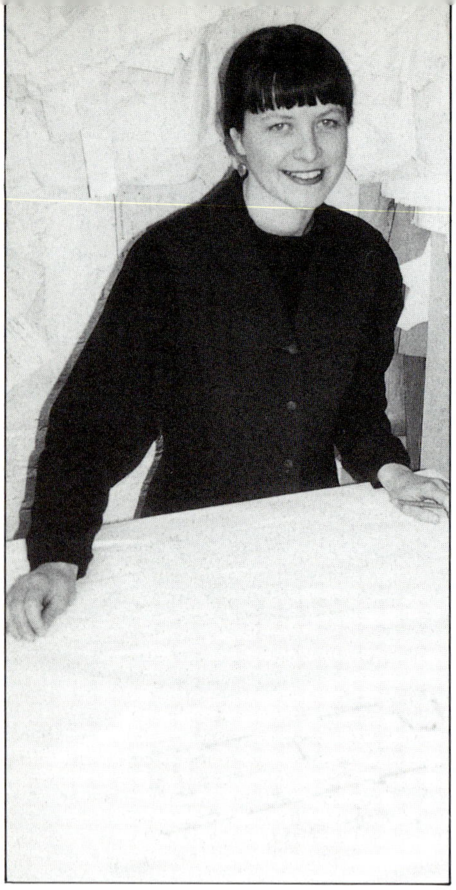

PATTERN MAKER

Each of Betty's designs comes to life through the skills of the **pattern maker, Jacquie Bounsall.** She explains:

'Betty and Lisa, her assistant, go through fabric swatches (examples of materials) and Lisa orders the fabrics with which we'll make the samples. She makes up "storyboards" to show the colour stories, the combinations of colours and patterns in each range. Betty is likely to start with a strong element, such as the woven straw she has used for jackets and shorts, and work a theme around that. That gives a strong feeling for the way the collection will go and helps me with my eventual interpretation of her sketches. You have to get on the same wavelength as the designer so that you know the overall look she's aiming at. My assistant and I work from Betty's sketches to produce patterns that are as near as possible to the sketches. We use either plain paper or "spot and cross" and draft the piece out. We may be able to adapt a pattern from a previous season (some pattern makers use "blocks", adapting standard shapes – others work totally from scratch.) Speed is essential, so I tend to adapt some pieces and combine them with new ones. We have only a few months to produce a large collection.

'When I've drafted the pattern out, I cut out the pieces and give them to Ann, our sample machinist, to produce a "toile" – the garment made up in a cloth which has similarities to the one we eventually intend to use. This is simply to give us an idea of whether the shape is right and will work. Someone tries it on, or we put it on the dummy, and Betty, Lisa and I will be critical about it, noting any changes necessary in size or pattern – lowering pockets, for instance, or changing the cut of the shoulder or the shape of the collar. Sometimes we draw the alterations on to the toile with a pen, or we may pin tape on to indicate the changes.

'It's very rare that a first toile is absolutely right, but it should be perfect by the second. If you get to a third toile, you need to start thinking seriously about whether you're in the right job!'

Jacquie and her assistant produce around 75 patterns each season. Each one is rarely made up in just one cloth. Some jackets, for example, may be produced in five totally different cloths, so the pattern may have to be amended for each one, to take into account their different weights or trimmings. There are also different colourways – samples, from which the buyers choose, are likely to be in three alternative colours. As the sample-making process continues, Jacquie constantly refines patterns and checks that the making up suits the cloth. Each pattern has a drawing and specification sheet of the processes the machinist must go through, which stay with it right until the model tries on the finished garment. It lists all the components (including the trimmings) and acts as a guide for future manufacture.

Betty then chooses and places the buttons on the samples (a button can totally alter the look of a garment) and the sample-making process is almost complete. It remains for Jacquie to send a card copy of the pattern to a freelance pattern grader who translates all the different pieces into the required sizes.

WAYS IN

You can start as a trainee pattern maker in the clothing industry at 16 years old, with few or no academic qualifications, working your way up. You can then continue your studies via day or block release or a full-time course. You may choose to follow a City and Guilds Clothing Craft 460 Certificate, with the option of Wholesale Garment Making or Handcraft Tailoring; the BTEC Certificate, HNC, Diploma or HND in Clothing Manufacture; or the SCOTVEC equivalents in Clothing. BA or BSc degrees in Clothing Design, Clothing Studies, Fashion and so on which include modules in pattern making are also a good way in.

Jacquie left school at 16 but knew she wanted to work in the fashion industry. She took art A level at an evening class, and followed a foundation year at Brighton with a Fashion Design course at St. Martin's College of Art, specialising in knitwear design. After working for top knitwear designer Patricia Roberts and selling her own designs at Covent Garden, she went back to college for an intensive six-month pattern cutting course. A job as pattern cutter for Ally Capellino lasted for five enjoyable years before her move to Betty Jackson, which was to offer her greater scope.

Pattern cutters are as important to the design process as designers. They can be highly creative people, often with a similar educational background to the designer. The rapport between them is of paramount importance for the success of the ultimate design, so personality plays a significant role. College entry requirements vary enormously, according to the course, but the resultant qualification is not a guarantee of a job – as with all areas of the fashion industry, couple your course with as wide a practical experience as you can.

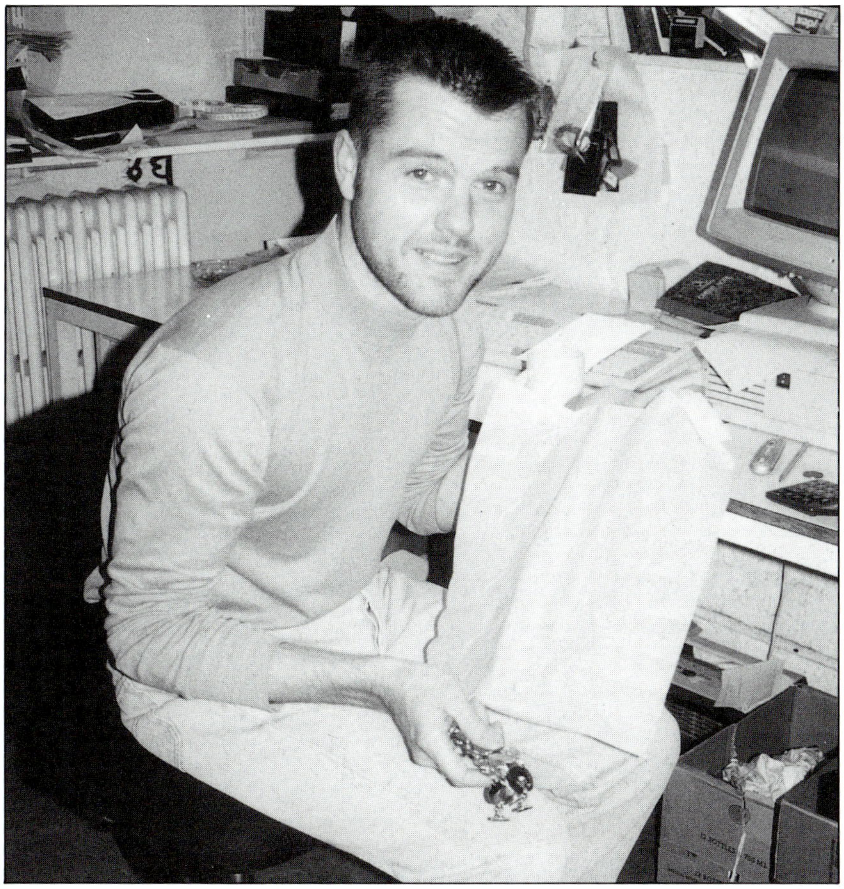

PRODUCTION MANAGER

The Production Department is the financial heart of a business like Betty Jackson. Once the samples have been made and the buyers have ordered the clothes they want to sell in their shops, their orders come down to the production department where they are processed together and put onto computer disk. **Sue Hollywood** is **Production Manager.** Together with **John Fairlie,** who concentrates on the accessories, she runs the department:

'I have a costing book, which gives me details of fabric, trimmings, buttons and so on. The quantities sold of each of these elements are fed into the computer, and it tells us how much we need to order for manufacture. It also prints out dockets showing the style, colour and quantity required in each size, for us to send with the fabric to the factories. It's our job to negotiate prices and delivery dates for fabrics and trimmings before faxing the orders through.

'Jacquie gives me the graded patterns and I do a plan for each factory, allocating the work. Some specialise, just making jackets, for instance, or only making up stretch Lycra for us. I work out prices and negotiate those with the factory. They then have an idea of what we expect them to produce over the next few months. Meanwhile, we wait for the fabric to come in, then put the patterns and trimmings with it and deliver it to the factories.'

Sue's responsibilities don't end there – she also has to keep an eye on quality and deal with day-to-day problems, chasing up the factories for delivery, dealing with faulty garments and putting through invoices.

WAYS IN

Both Sue and John have a fashion background – Sue took art and needlework A levels and began as an invoice clerk with designer Zandra Rhodes; John studied Fashion at college. Numeracy is obviously important in the job, as well as computer literacy – and an interest in (and preferably experience of) fashion is vital in this competitive world. Most BTEC and degree courses in fashion have elements of production within them.

The manufacturing process is where all those hours of hard work by designers finally take form for the general public to benefit.

Once the designer has done a drawing and finalised the design in a toile, the pattern maker translates that into a pattern and the manufacturing process can begin. Betty Jackson has her own pattern maker for small factories to make up her designs. Large manufacturers employ their own pattern makers/pattern cutters.

In a large company, the pattern maker is a pattern technologist who is responsible for all aspects of pattern cutting and grading (producing the pattern in different sizes, making sure that the proportions remain the same), the pattern lays (how the pattern is to be laid out on the material most economically), and the samples. They cut the patterns using a pattern block as a guide.

Once they've made the pattern, the pattern cutter may have to make slight alterations after an initial pilot run, before it is graded into the different sizes needed for mass production. Grading is done by pasting the pattern onto a computerised 'digitising table' and allotting it 'rule numbers'. These are fed into the computer using a cursor pen and the pattern is automatically graded.

When it has been plotted out on paper, the pattern is laid onto layers of fabric for cutting. But before it can be cut, the lay planner must make sure that the fabric is being cut in the most economical way, making the best use of the material. It's just like a puzzle – but a great deal of money could depend on whether you get it right or not! In a large factory, all this is computerised, with details of the numbers, sizes and shapes of the pattern pieces being fed in, digested and organised into the optimum arrangement. Once the lay planner feels that the best 'lay' has been achieved, that plan (or 'marker') is stored on disc. Computerised equipment is used to plot a full-scale copy onto heat-fixed paper and from there it is sent to the cutting room, to be ironed onto the layers of fabric waiting to be cut. It's also the lay planner's job to calculate the fabric costs for the management by working out the length of each lay and dividing by the number of garments to get an average.

New technology has revolutionised production in larger factories, used not only for pattern grading and lay planning, but also to assist designers with colour planning in the initial stages.

In a small factory, it's a completely different matter. Designers like Betty Jackson, who don't need thousands of garments, use smaller companies to produce a few clothes for a limited number of outlets.

MANUFACTURING

CORTESSA is a small, family-run business in east London which makes up for designers such as Betty Jackson, Caroline Charles, Workers for Freedom, Whistles and Hobbs. It's 20 years since **Andrew Fearon's** father first started the business, and there have been some pretty tough times. The competition within the industry is tremendous, so prices must be kept down, quality strictly maintained and delivery deadlines met. Andrew himself picks up the fabric, together with the patterns (they use an outside cutter) and the sample (if there is one!) which shows them what the finished garment should look like. Andrew learnt his trade from his parents, who started the business, backed up by a course at the London College of Fashion, and now applies it in the homely and happy atmosphere of the small factory which he runs with his mother.

Ron Pether, a **cutter,** studies his cutting dockets for details of pattern, style and sizes, lays up the pattern onto the waiting layers of fabric, marking round them with chalk, and cuts out using an electric 'straight knife', capable of cutting several hundred layers of fabric at once. He acknowledges that there's quite a skill in the job:

'It's just like working out a jigsaw when you plan how to lay the pattern out – and you need a steady hand to cut them.'

Once it's cut, the fabric is sorted out and marked up so that the machinists will know the right and wrong sides. All the pieces are overlocked on a machine so that they don't fray. After any fusing (interfacing) is applied they are sorted into bundles together with explanatory tickets, labels and any trimmings.

If it's a complex style, **Doris Jones,** a skilled **machinist,** makes up a sample to demonstrate how it should be put together. Her sample will go back to the designer to be checked if there are any queries – it's then the job of the machinist to take a bundle and piece the garment together. Doris doubles as supervisor:

'I get the girls working, check that they're doing O.K. and help them with any problems. You have to be diplomatic and patient – but there's a very happy atmosphere here.'

At Cortessa, the machinists 'work through', which means that they make a complete garment at a time. In larger factories, machinists are likely to concentrate on one aspect of making up – such as just sewing collars or sleeves.

This 'making through' is one of the elements which **Naseem Fazin, machinist,** most enjoys about the job:

'It's so much more interesting and rewarding than doing one thing all the time and never seeing the finished results. There's a lot of variety in my work. I may be sewing on buttons, making button holes or overlocking, or I could be making up a complete garment. I came here straight from school on a YTS and learnt on-the-job – and I was happy to stay on at the end! I move around, working on a different task each day, and it's very satisfying that way, to see what you've achieved.'

The machinists work a flexible day, between the hours of 7.30 and 5.00. Some are paid hourly; others are paid 'piece work', according to their rate of production.

After machining, the clothes are marked up for buttons and buttonholes before moving on for hand-finishing – that means sewing on buttons, shoulder pads and any other details. From there it's a short step to pressing, where **Paula Michael** and **Sam Antwi** who are both **pressers,** are nifty with an iron:

'It's an extra heavy iron which is connected to a steam boiler to produce more steam than the domestic version, so you get a better finish. It takes practice, but you soon become quick. And there's no need to worry about scorching these beautiful designer fabrics ... the irons have nylon shields on them, so you can't do any harm!'

Andrew Fearon points out that they are all very aware of the high standards demanded of them. They take pride in the quality they produce – everything is continually checked – and they all agree on how rewarding it is to see their clothes featured in magazines or on catwalk models on T.V.!

Andrew Fearon

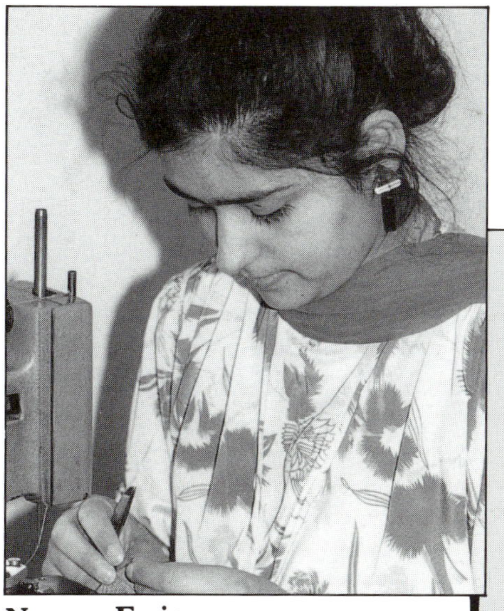

Naseem Fazin

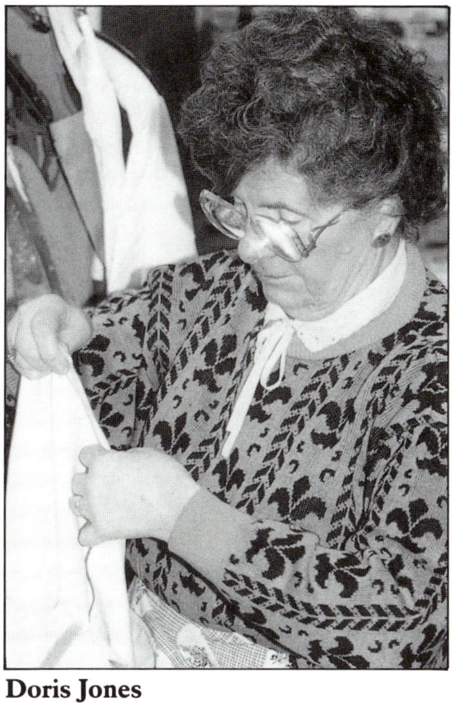

Doris Jones

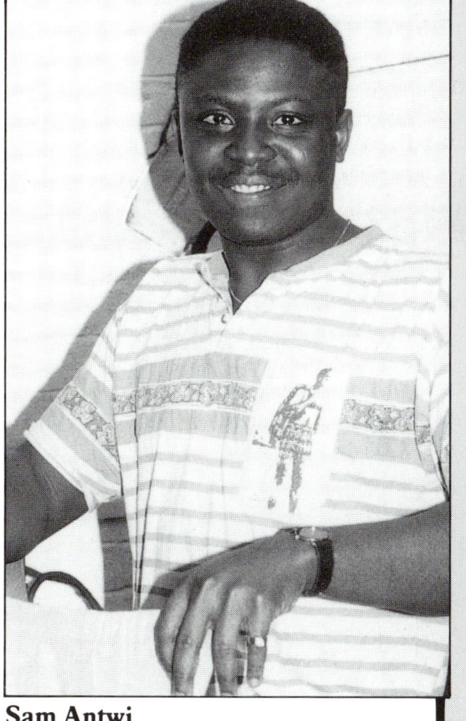

Sam Antwi

Ron Pether

WAYS IN

These manufacturing jobs don't require any academic qualifications, but they do demand a certain aptitude. Andrew Fearon normally only recruits machinists and pressers – most other jobs are the result of internal promotions. You'll hear of vacancies by word of mouth or see them advertised in the local press. Factories often put a sign up outside their premises if there are any vacancies; alternatively write directly to the firm.

There are various courses which relate to clothing manufacture, including the City and Guilds Clothing Craft 460 Certificate, BTEC and SCOTVEC Certificates and Diplomas at various levels, and the Clothing Skills Awards, which were launched in 1988 and are approved as a National Vocational Qualification (NVQ). They were initially introduced for machinists but are now open to all clothing employees. The Clothing and Allied Products Industry Training Board (CAPITB) is developing NVQs for pressers, cutters, quality controllers, clothing machine mechanics and technicians, instructors, supervisors, designers and managers.

FASHION RETAILING

The retail side of the fashion industry is the area with the most public contact ... every one of us buys clothes, and each of us is familiar with the face the retail industry presents to its customers.

Retail jobs with a fashion bias include buying, merchandising/planning and display/visual merchandising, as well as sales (covered in depth in 'Working In the Retail Industry').

BUYER

How would you feel about jetting around the world, stopping off in Milan or Paris ... or perhaps New York to view the world's most desirable fashion collections, spending thousands of pounds of someone else's money as you go! Sounds wonderfully glamorous, doesn't it? But the realities of fashion buying are far removed from jet-setting ease. It's a job which requires hard work and dedication – a willingness to work late, to give up your weekends and to up sticks and go wherever you're sent at the drop of a hat.

Buying is a risk business. A buyer needs to be aware of developing trends and able to spot from them which 'look' will be the next success story. Decisions to buy are based on solid facts, not purely on the buyer's whim ... don't forget that if the store isn't stocking what the customer wants to buy, they're not going to be around for long.

Amanda Verdan is the **Director of Buying** at Harvey Nichols, a job which she came to via selling experience with Fortnum and Mason, an exciting and exacting job working for designer Jean Muir, and a progression from accessories buyer to Head of Womenswear buying with Harvey Nichols:

'Buyers who can see talent in its raw form, spotting potential in unknown designers, are few and far between. But that's the secret of success – knowing when something is special and making sure your store has it first. What the buyer does is to view collections and then extract elements of them so that the end result is a department which has a cohesive look. A look that interprets the many different fashion elements so that the customer will digest and desire it. That skill of mentally editing down a collection is an essential part of the buyer's task. All buyers work to a tight budget. Before they embark on their buying, the previous figures will have been analysed by department, style, brand and garment and the directors will have approved a buying strategy, so the buyer will then know whether a certain style is likely to sell well and what proportion of each garments to buy – a certain ratio of jackets to skirts, for instance, in specified quantities. With experience, buyers get to know which companies are best for certain things – one designer may use the best quality fabric with consistently good cut and the most competitive price in, say, outwear, whilst another may produce the best jackets.'

Amanda points out that it's an ever-changing business – and it's the buyer's job to respond to this by working closely with the planners or merchandisers to make sure that the right clothes are being stocked at the right time. If, for instance, a new trend is emerging half way through the season, the buyer may have to go out and buy more to cope with the demand. As Amanda explains:

'That flexibility is essential. They need to be able to buy in quickly or get rid of something that isn't selling. They're constantly working in the past, present *and* future. Buyers in the store need to have the same philosophy, a view of the store's image which complies with the directors' view and that of the consumer. They have to buy carefully in order to perpetuate our quality image so that the customer will trust the store and the products.'

Before the buying even starts, Amanda and her colleagues will have conducted a colour analysis for each of the fashion floors, so that when the new season's clothes are in place, there will be that unmistakeable look of style and direction, rather than a jumbled mass of rainbow colours. The idea is to make shopping as easy and as pleasurable as possible for the customer, in an environment that is pleasing to the eye. All buyers will then be briefed as to the colour palette for which they're buying. Throughout the buying season (which lasts for several months), there will be numerous meetings to check that all is going to plan.

Buyers watch the couture shows around the world and also visit showrooms of ready-to-wear companies, perhaps taking a whole day to view a collection in all its colours before deciding on the combination of outfits to buy. They don't place an order there and then, since many thousands of pounds may be at stake and mistakes are expensive. Instead, they return to the store and spend two or three days making sure that they have the right balance of outfits. The final numbers will be computerised and checked by the Director of Buying before orders are sent out. One of the key requirements is to make sure that deliveries appear at the right time so that the square footage in the shop allocated to a specific garment is always filled. It's a constant juggling act.

Comparative shopping is also important – buyers need to visit other stores to see what they are selling, whether there are new names which would sell well and how their clothes are displayed. In fashion, it's vital to stay ahead.

WAYS IN

Buyers need to be decisive and have confidence in their own decisions. Numeracy is important, as is the ability to envisage clothes in another size or colour and how their selecion is going to look on the shop floor. A good colour sense is important, coupled with the ability to put clothes together with style to make an outfit. Amanda concludes:

'We look for people who are down-to-earth and professional in their approach, yet able to communicate well with people in a friendly way – they are, after all, ambassadors for the store.'

Most buying opportunities are within stores and shop groups. Different stores and groups (such as Miss Selfridge, Marks and Spencer, the Burton Group, House of Fraser, Harrods, Fenwicks and Dickens and Jones) have their own training schemes, with varying requirements. It is advisable to contact them direct.

MERCHANDISER

Merchandisers are employed by larger retail stores and groups. It is their job to work with the buyer to make sure that the shop can supply the clothes the public are going to want to buy, in the right quantities. The merchandiser or planner works out how much money should be spent by the buyer, based on the sales needed. That will then be broken down into figures for each type of garment – so much for jackets, so much for skirts, and so on. Once the buyer has chosen the fashions to be sold, the merchandiser's job is to make sure that they are in the right place, at the right time.

Large organisations like the Burton Group employ teams of buyers and merchandisers who specialise in specific areas. The buyer orders the clothes and passes that information to the merchandising team. An allocator processes the order, computerising the information. The order is sent to the supplier and a record kept of when delivery is due. It's the job of the assistant merchandiser to chase up deliveries – there are often hitches, but obviously the store needs a complete range at a time to be able to display and sell the goods satisfactorily. It's the assistant merchandiser's job to get tough!

Once deliveries have arrived, they go to the central warehouse where they are checked off and, in the case of a group like Burton's made available for delivery to the store for which they've been selected. An outline plan of each store's needs will have been based on historical information and projected sales figures, worked out by each department, brand and category of garment.

Liz Herrod is the **Senior Planning Manager** of Womenswear at Harvey Nichols, a title which recently replaced that of **Senior Merchandiser.** She first applied for retail training with the Burton Group after a degree in psychology which left her knowing that she *didn't* want to be a psychologist! Liz had worked for John Lewis during the vacations and was interested in what went on behind the scenes:

'I began as an allocator, working under the merchandiser and in charge of the distribution of stock, monitoring it and making sure that it was sent to the right shop as well as recording weekly sales figures. It's a fairly junior post, but mostly staffed now by graduates or people with A levels or equivalent – promotion prospects are good. I gradually moved up the ranks, from senior allocator to assistant merchandiser and senior merchandiser, moving between departments within that to gain an overall view of different garment types and how to deal with each one. For example, you would expect to sell less volume in formal wear than in T-shirts, which naturally affects the buying of cloth and size of orders. I moved to Harvey Nichols as a merchandiser and have developed my career from there.'

It's at quite a junior level in the merchandiser's career that they learn how to react to market forces, calculating how many of a garment they expect to sell and how quickly. From that information they can work out when to send the next batch of stock to the stores. As Liz explains:

'The job involves reacting to whether stock is selling or not and redistributing it to those outlets that need it. If stock is late from the manufacturers, or there's a problem with it, we're entitled to cancel it altogether – a loophole which we have to use when a line simply isn't selling and so our income is down, reducing the buying budget. If sales are much higher than expected, that generates more money and the merchandiser reacts by ordering more. This can be a problem for some shops though, who order six months in advance from ranges. It is quite likely that we wouldn't be able to repeat an order – in which case we calculate what we should have ordered and use the information for next season. The multiples, who may be buying 10,000 of a garment made specifically for them, are more likely to be able to order more direct from a factory.'

Analytical skills are something that a merchandiser learns with experience, watching how well stock and sales are performing in comparison with each other, making allowances for events which will dramatically affect sales – the Cup Final, for instance, is said to decimate Burton's sales figures on that particular Saturday because no-one goes shopping! Harvey Nichols was hit by the Gulf War, since many of their customers were not travelling and there were few foreign visitors in London. The merchandisers and planners have to forecast as much as possible to make sure that they have the right stock, and react instantly to changing influences.

Liz's job now involves forward planning, liaising with the buying department and looking at profit forecasts for the store according to each floor, its area and brands. The first floor, for instance, sells top designer fashions. This product has to make a profit, but it is also an important draw for customers who will then spend money in other departments.

The challenge for Liz and her colleagues is in keeping ahead of the game in a competitive world – and in remedying the situation when sales figures are down ... the buzz comes from seeing all the hard work come to fruition when the figures are up! The beauty of the job is that it combines the fun world of fashion with the challenge of running a business.

WAYS IN

There are opportunities at all levels. A number of fashion degree and diploma courses now incorporate business administration and marketing; many business studies courses have options relevant to retail. Numeracy, literacy and computer literacy are the most important criteria looked for by an employer, coupled with an awareness of fashion trends.

Large stores and multiples have graduate training schemes for careers in retailing, but all are over-subscribed. The Burton Group, for example, recently had 1400 applications for the 30 places on its Corporate Buying and Merchandising scheme; Selfridges attracted 2000 for a similar number of places, Marks and Spencer three times as many!

It's worth noting, though, that even after a graduate training scheme there is no guarantee of employment – and salary, perks and promotion are all based on individual merit.

DISPLAY/VISUAL MERCHANDISER

You've probably heard it said that people 'buy with their eyes' – and you'll know yourself how much more alluring is a stunning shop window than a dull pile of boxes or a random heap of unappealing pullovers. Visual merchandising – displaying goods for sale, either in windows or inside a store – has the power to attract customers and make them want to buy a product or an image.

In the case of Harvey Nichols' windows, masterminded by the dynamic **Mary Portas,** a **visual merchandiser,** they have the power to draw gasps of admiration, screams of laughter and stares of disbelief. Harvey Nichols has become famous for its window displays, fantastic theatrical creations which are unrivalled in their ingenuity, originality and style, and recognised by having won every available award. Mary had wanted to be an actress, and studied at drama school, but family misfortunes led to her leaving early:

'I had a temporary job over the summer and helped the guy there with designing exhibition stands. It appealed so much that I went off to art school and took a course in display and design. It covered perspective drawing, graphic design and window display – it's no longer a question of draping a few clothes over a stiff-looking mannequin. You have to be creative and artistic, with an eye for colour and design as well as the ability to put clothes together and make a statement. I spent two weeks at Harvey Nichols on work experience and just fell in love with it.'

The competition to get work after college is tremendous. Mary was advised to take her portfolio to Harrods since Harvey Nichols weren't recruiting, and she rang constantly to ask if there was a vacancy. Eventually her persistence paid off and she worked there for two-and-a-half years, starting as a trainee, 'picking up pins and sweeping floors', and progressing to dressing:

'I was dressing windows at Way In in Harrods when a guy asked me to dress some shops in the King's Road. I picked up several jobs like that and finally gave up my job at Harrods to freelance for a year. I used to design the windows and make the props in my

back garden! I had really enjoyed the fashion work at Harrods so when I heard that the fashion chain Wallis (who at that time had the best windows) had a vacancy for a fashion stylist, I snapped it up. My job was to design a window display, which was then sent to all their shops throughout the country, to be adapted by them.'

The management side of the business attracted Mary, so when she was 24 she applied for the job of Display Manager for Top Shop at London's Oxford Circus branch, organising a display team of six. It wasn't long before she was in charge of the display of all of their 150 stores, but then the recession bit and creative display dropped in the company's list of priorities. Fortuitously, Harvey Nichols was owned by the same group and it was suggested that Mary move there as Head of Display. She now has dual responsibility for Sales Promotions and Visual Merchandising:

'I run a whole set of windows and interiors, managing a team of 16, working in conjunction with the Buying Director and the Sales Director to modernise the new menswear department, planning the placement of products and creating visual themes within the departments, pulling it all together so that there's a cohesive design. The Buying Director, the Sales Director and I work closely together, resolving the problems of combining the hard facts of numbers of outfits per square foot with the visual appeal of the sales area.'

Mary's task starts with the twice yearly collections, visiting as many fashion shows as possible in London, Paris, New York and Milan, then getting together with Amanda, the Buying Director, to discuss the key looks for the season and work out colour themes. Mary plans five or six weeks in advance, but various landmarks on the calendar will influence the theme – in 1992, for example, February heralded a spring look of suits for women. Mary had the idea of using the city newspaper, the Financial Times, which is printed on pink paper, to form the link between city suits and femininity (in its colour, pink). As the creative process progressed, she came up with designs for a series of window displays based on giant sculptures made from hundreds of copies of the Financial Times. March is London Fashion Week, when the windows normally salute British designers; April and May reflect the high society season, with themes of Wimbledon, Ascot and Henley. Christmas is bound to have an influence on the displays – and so are the New Year and Summer Sales. The basic starting point may be elementary, but the resultant design is innovative and original. Mary explains:

'You have to create some sort of theatre with a window, that will make people stop. We're never too targeted – we don't need to create a particular image to attract a certain sort of customer. Consequently, we can produce something that's completely different and attention-grabbing.'

After the design has been thought up, Mary makes a cardboard model of each window, showing exactly how it will look, and takes it along to the Managing Director, to discuss with him. She costs it out (display teams must work to a budget) and discusses it with her immediate team of Display Manager and two stylists. Between them, they finalise ideas before calling in the prop makers (carpenters and artists) who will make the set up off-site. The team instals the finished displays, often working well into the evening – and waits for public reaction! It's this feedback that provides the rewards. To watch people stop in the street and admire your work is guaranteed to make you feel good.

WAYS IN

You need a good standard of general education, with an artistic ability. Most full-time courses require three GCSEs or their equivalent, including art and English. It's usual to complete some college training before you start work; people who are trained in-store often gain college qualifications on a day-release basis.

There are two examining bodies which offer courses in display – the British Display Society (BDS) and BTEC. The BDS requirements range from no academic qualifications for a 16 year old on the General Certificate Grade 1 to a BTEC/SCOTVEC diploma for the National Diploma (Final Level). BTEC offers Certificate and Diploma courses, all requiring three GCSEs or their equivalent.

You may have heard of public relations ('P.R.') and thought it sounded glamorous – or you may not have the faintest idea what it entails! A public relations officer (P.R. for short) promotes the work of the client, giving the latest news to the media and ensuring that the public get to hear about it. They may also give marketing advice, researching what the public wants and passing that on to the client in terms of suggested strategy.

Advertising and promotions may also be handled by the P.R. , or an advertising executive – either 'in-house' or by an agency. Advertising forms an important part of a firm's strategy. Harvey Nichols, for example, spends 75% of its large advertising budget on advertising womenswear by the specific designers' ranges it sells, with a further 15% on menswear advertising. Coupled with in-store promotions, it is the most effective way to market the store, its image and its products. The advertising campaigns are planned six months in advance, when the director of advertising and promotions meets with the buying director and the sales director to decide on key looks and the names they want to promote. The advertising space is then booked in the magazines by the publicity team and the ads themselves designed. This strategy is backed up by promotional activity, inviting the press into the store for previews, linking up with magazines for evening promotions with their readers, organising free gifts, and inviting guests to prestigious venues to promote Harvey Nichols and specific products. In the case of smaller stores, promotional activity will involve using imagination to create events which will cost little or nothing but be effective in publicising the company or the product.

Fashion P.R.s either work in-house, employed by a company's public relations department (or, in a smaller organisation, as an individual member of the business team) to publicise the company – perhaps in the press office of a department store or a clothing manufacturer; or they work in a P.R. consultancy or agency, working on behalf of several clients – promoting a certain designer, for example, or shops, accessories or cosmetics.

Lynne Franks Ltd. is one of London's foremost P.R. agencies and their influence is all around you. The relaunch of Brylcreem in the '80s, for instance, was a Lynne Franks success story, as were campaigns like the Next Directory and the Swatch watch. Clients range from Littlewoods to Lenny Henry, with a hardcore in the fashion industry.

PUBLIC RELATIONS AND ADVERTISING

ACCOUNT EXECUTIVE

Gordon Hagan is an **account executive** at Lynne Franks Ltd. A degree in economics and politics may sound an unusual route into fashion P.R., but in fact Gordon's interest in fashion led to his leaving university after two years and starting work full-time as a fashion buyer for some friends who had a shop:

'It was great fun and good experience working with clothes. I knew I wanted to get into fashion P.R., and sent a C.V. here. I was asked to come for a chat, and then I came back for an interview with the fashion director.'

Gordon was asked to write a sample press release and ultimately got the job of Trainee Account Executive, giving him the opportunity to build up his fashion P.R. experience:

'I was trained here, on-the-job, and sent on a couple of courses to master skills like word processing. Initially, the trainee's role is to support the existing team. On the mundane side, that can involve updating mailing lists, filing and checking goods for photography. As you gain experience, so you spend more time phoning the press and talking to clients.

'The main basis of the work is to forge good relationships with the media, judging where best to place a story and what would interest each journalist. The aim then is to give them information which will ensure that my clients have good media coverage and so remain in the public eye. It includes print journalism (the national press, consumer mags like *The Face* and *ID*, and the trade press), radio and television – the contact is made either over the phone or via press releases which must be concise and precise to target specific information. Accounts could involve a particular launch, like a range of clothing or the opening of a new shop, or it may mean more general publicity. People forget very quickly, so you need to keep reminding them of your client's name to keep the profile high. What you're doing is fanning the flames.

'We also host events. For instance, one of my accounts now is St. Christopher's Place, an up-market fashion area of London. We organised a big party there to celebrate 75 years of the covers of 'Vogue' magazine. It was a high profile fashion event with celebrities and pop stars. I had to contact their agents and find out who was in town, whose record was currently doing well (no point in having someone who's going down – that would create the wrong image) and who would be able to come. Having arranged the event, journalists and editors had to be contacted and invited to the party which acted as a preview of the exhibition covers. There was also a readers' evening for *Vogue* readers, and a fashion show. It was exciting but hard work.

'It's a very stimulating job, but the nature of it is that you can never do enough, so you make constant demands on yourself, working quickly and intensively – that's exhilarating and exhausting!'

Fashion P.R. isn't all glamour. They tend to work long hours (often from 9am until 7pm, five days a week), and they have to be prepared to work late to get a job finished. They need to speak well, be sincere and be interested in people and their work – if they're not, that will convey itself to the client and the press ... and that spells disaster!

WAYS IN

Most fashion P.R.s have some fashion experience behind them – work in the fashion industry is normally considered more relevant than previous P.R. experience. It is often possible for students to get work experience in a P.R. agency – an invaluable way in. Lynne Franks Ltd., for instance, have several students at any one time, either arranged in conjunction with a school or as a result of an individual sending their C.V. to the office manager.

There are no prescribed qualifications for working in fashion P.R. other than a good standard of education and personal attributes such as efficiency, tact, immaculate appearance, enthusiasm and ambition.

Although not essential, a CAM (Communication, Advertising and Marketing Education Foundation) Certificate in Communication Studies is a useful qualification. For entry to their Part 1 Certificate, candidates must be at least 18 years old with either:

- a degree or two A levels and at least three GCSEs or equivalent, including English language;
- have been in full-time employment in a relevant area of the communications business for at least one year and have five good GCSEs, including English language;
- have passed the London Chamber of Commerce and Industry Third Level Group Diploma in Advertising, Marketing and Public Relations or the International Advertising Association Basic Certificate in Advertising, or a CAM-recognised foundation course.

Other courses in P.R. are available – the Public Relations Consultants Association sponsors training courses for member companies' employees and the Institute of Public Relations organises specialist short courses and practical workshops for members of the Institute.

FASHION EDITOR

If you want to break into fashion journalism, you need more than an ability to write and an eye for clothes ... it takes perseverance, determination and an element of luck.

Vivienne Palmer, a **fashion editor,** always knew that she wanted a career in fashion. With nine O levels and two A levels, she joined a training scheme at a department store in Kingston, to become a fashion buyer. After only a few months, Vivienne realised that it wasn't for her, and began to look for a job in fashion journalism:

'For ten months I wrote to magazines, asking for jobs, and eventually I became Fashion and Beauty Assistant on a teenage magazine called *Fab 208*. It wasn't quite as glamorous as it sounds – I was mostly general dogsbody – but the Fashion and Beauty Editor included me in her work, taking me on photographic sessions and letting me write the occasional article, so I learnt as I went along. Eventually, she used to leave me in charge when she went on holiday. It was good all-round experience. After *Fab,* I worked on a couple of other teenage magazines as Fashion and Beauty Editor before moving to *Woman's Realm* as Assistant Beauty Editor. I knew that I wanted to be a fashion editor, but I also realised that I needed to gain experience on a large publication first.'

From there, via the job of Assistant Fashion Editor on *Prima,* Vivienne is now Fashion Editor at *Options,* a well established and glossy monthly magazine ... a far cry from the days of *Fab 208.* With Jane, her assistant, Vivienne runs the fashion department at *Options,* with virtual autonomy:

'I go to the "collections" twice a year in London and Paris to see the shows given for the press by the fashion houses. They give me a good idea of what is going to be in the shops – the future trends and shapes that will be likely to have an impact on the high street. From them, I will form an idea of what I would like to include in the three fashion features I'm responsible for each month. I plan two months at a time with the editor of the magazine, working three to four months ahead. For instance, I have just written a "white story" for a summer issue, I'm currently working on a feature using pyjamas for outdoor wear, and I'm about to go off to Barbados for a week to do a shoot (photography) for four different features.

'The designer shows give me an overall view of key trends. I then use their clothes, mixed with clothes from high street stores, to produce the look I want. It's important to remember who your readers are, their likely lifestyle and what sort of money they are going to be willing to spend on clothes.'

For *Options,* that means a range of prices to give a look that's stylish but still comparatively young. The skill comes in mixing the work of different designers together successfully. When Vivienne has decided on the look she wants, she writes the story, working from the detailed notes and sketches she makes at the shows and checking through the hundreds of transparencies taken by the photographer, not only at the London and Paris collections, but also in New York and Milan. A combination of phone calls and appointments with designers and P.R. agencies ensures that the clothes Vivienne has chosen can be borrowed and sent to the office for the specific feature (which will either be shot in a studio or on location). It all sounds so simple, but in fact it can be a nightmare! Every garment (and there may be hundreds for a location shoot) must be carefully logged in, so that they know where it comes from – and where and when it has to go back! Other publications may be waiting to borrow the clothes, so Vivienne and Jane must be supremely organised, to make sure that they keep each item for the minimum amount of time. And it's not just clothes ... show designers and manufacturers bring in polaroids of their new designs so that a choice may be made from those; and Vivienne does all her own 'styling' for the photographs, so she may have to go out to the shops to look for a 'prop' such as a giant urn – or an accessory or piece of underwear to match exactly with something else. It's all very time consuming.

Before a trip, they have to liaise with the photographer about the models and make sure they are booked. That could mean spending a morning looking at albums of models in agencies, trying to find the right ones – it is quite likely to involve flying models out from Paris or Milan to meet them. A recent trip took them to Kenya for a week, photographing, among others, Betty Jackson's clothes. It sounds hassle free, enticing and, frankly, a bit of a holiday, but in fact there were problems at the airport, which cost them precious time and money; they had to be up 4 each morning so that they could make the most of the marvellous Kenyan early morning light for photographs at 6.30, before it became too hot and hazy; afternoons were spent moving to another location before the later afternoon shoot; and evenings were spent wading through all the ironing for the following day! The organisation required for a trip like that is immense, especially because if you forget something, you can't just nip back and get it. All the clothes are 'styled' first in the office before they leave the country, making sure that they know exactly what will make an outfit. At *Options*, with only two of them in the fashion department, this is a particularly hectic time. Some other, larger magazines may have four in the fashion department, with someone whose job it is simply to book the models or set up the location shots.

'It's lovely to go to all these exotic places, but it's very stressful. You always have to worry about whether you're running out of money, if the weather and the light will be right, and whether the shots will be exactly what you want when you get back home. You're quite likely to be hungry because you miss breakfast (the hotel doesn't serve it at 4am) and you're too tired to enjoy it when you get to dinner! When we get back to London, we send all the clothes back, write the copy (the story) and the captions for each photo and check details like the retail cost of the clothes. After that, it's a case of finalising the layout with the Art Department and, when everything has been checked, typeset and re-checked, waiting to see the results when it's finally printed. Meanwhile the whole process has already started again ... sometimes it feels relentless! It's very pressurised, with constant deadlines to meet, designers and P.R. agencies to see, editorial meetings to attend, press receptions to go to, locations to check and shoots to organise. You have to be on the ball. The up-side is that it's not in any way a mundane 9-5 office job. You have to be dedicated ... if you're the sort of person who wants to leave at 6 o'clock , forget it. If we've got a deadline to meet, Jane and I may come in at 7am and still be here at 10 o'clock at night. We may even come in on a Saturday. It can be exciting and exhausting, it carries terrific responsibility – but it's also interesting and unpredictable.'

WAYS IN

There are more opportunities for fashion journalists on magazines than newspapers. Not only are there the consumer magazines like *Options, 19* and *Vogue,* bought by the general public; there are also trade magazines such as *DR – the Fashion Business, Fashion Weekly* and ***International Textiles.*** You are unlikely to see first jobs on magazines advertised. Editors and personnel departments get so many letters asking for a job that they can normally choose from them. If you are writing to a magazine or newspaper, write a letter that is interesting, neat and polite and address it directly to the fashion editor. Remember that you will probably have to start as a secretary or editorial assistant, so typing/word processing skills will help.

You will normally need A levels or their equivalent or a degree. The London College of Fashion runs a two-year HND in Fashion Business, incorporating Fashion Writing, at the London College of Fashion; and St. Martin's College of Art runs a four-year BA (Hons) in Fashion, Promotion and Communication. Another way in is via a degree in fashion or, for trade magazines, business studies, backed up by an ability to write. For newspaper journalism, the National Council for the Training of Journalists (NCTJ) runs a one-year college pre-entry course – for entry, you need five GCSEs/S grades or equivalent or two AS levels and four GCSEs, or two A levels/H grades (one of them in English).

Some schools can arrange work experience with the fashion department of a magazine or newspaper which will give you a taste of the job before you pursue it any further.

FASHION PHOTOGRAPHY

It isn't easy to break into fashion photography. There are simply so many photographers that you have to be very good – and very determined – to succeed. Practically all fashion photographers are freelance, which means they must sell themselves and their work to fashion editors, art directors and other potential clients. Many have an agent (who usually takes a 25% commission). The agent will look after several photographers at once, in theory getting them the sort of work that suits them, with the right sort of client.

FREELANCE PHOTOGRAPHER

Martyn Thompson, now a successful **freelance fashion photographer,** read English at university before working in a variety of fashion and journalism related jobs:

'I did some freelance fashion designing and opened my own shop. Obviously, I needed promotional photography, so I started taking my own. I became really interested in the technical side ... why a certain shot was too dark or too light and how to correct it – what worked and what didn't. It was that unique combination of the artistic, aesthetic side and the technical expertise which really attracted me to the job. So my background was essentially fashion; other people choose a photographic route in, gaining their fashion experience later. Whichever you do, it's essential to have a keen interest in the two. It's no good simply being able to take good photographs without having strong ideas about what clothes, what looks you like and don't like. It's that individuality which will make people choose your work rather than someone else's. If you feel wishy washy about it, that will come over in the end result. For example, I don't like to photograph girls looking aggressive. I prefer a softer, more beautiful look – and clients know that when they choose me.

'It's important to have a goal in sight and work towards that. I would ultimately like to do some particular perfume ads, so I build up my portfolio with that end in mind. Many fashion photographers have a "signature", a distinct style which develops as they go along. It changes as you move on. You may spend six months photographing things in a certain way and then, just suddenly, decide to do something completely new. It could happen by accident – some lights could blow and affect the end result in a way which influences your future style – or it could be carefully thought out in advance.'

Fashion photographers rarely have their own studios nowadays. Most hire studios, equipment and lights, owning only their cameras. It costs a lot of money to run a studio – and when you're travelling around and not using it, you're wasting that money. Martyn has a full-time assistant who knows exactly how he likes to work and can set up the studio before Martyn arrives. He takes photographs for magazines, fashion P.R., catalogues and advertising agencies, all of which may contact him direct or his agent.

'Magazine work is more personal, when you're working with a fashion editor, hair and make-up people and the models to produce a personal picture which is an expression of what you want to do. Catalogue work is more constrained because there are certain details which need to be seen.

'I usually know in advance the sort of shots I'm likely to be taking. I plan what I'm going to do and brief my assistant so that he knows what to set up. Occasionally we may get a background, lights and model ready and decide it doesn't look right. That's when the phone calls begin to get other props or clothes sent in.

'When the model has had her hair and make-up done and is dressed, we're ready to shoot. It's important to build up a rapport with the model. Sometimes I know them already, but it's usually quite a quick process if the model is experienced.'

To shoot one magazine cover it may take a couple of hours. Usually, they take two or three at a time to make the best use of the studio and the models. It has to be a good, strong picture, so they may shoot 300 transparencies to make sure that they get what they want. The film then goes off to the lab to be developed. From that Martyn chooses 20 or so shots to take to the client.

'You have to be decisive – do you abandon a shoot if the weather is appalling, or wait for an improvement? Can you decide which shots from several hundred are the ones which will sell your work to an editor? You need to be patient and adaptable and cope with the emotional ups and downs. It's a 24 hour a day job in that you find yourself thinking about it all the time. I work odd, irregular hours – it could be every weekend for a month, or daily, 5am to 9pm on location. There are periods of intense work and others where I may not work at all for a couple of weeks. It's one of the hazards of being freelance and it makes me very difficult to live with! If you can't handle that sort of uncertainty, you may as well not bother!'

Before you set up, you need to build up a portfolio of your work to show prospective clients. It's a slow process and likely to be a difficult time financially, when you'll need the security of another job to see you through. You have to have the determination to ring up art directors and fashion editors, making appointments for them to see your work and give you their opinion. From there you can refine and redefine your style.

The Association of Fashion, Advertising and Editorial Photographers (AFAEP) suggests one of two routes:

- take a college course;
- get a job as a photographer's assistant and take a day-release or evening class at the same time.

Entry to each is highly competitive.

If you do a college course, give yourself a head start by doing as many work placements as you can before you leave.

College courses vary enormously in their content, so you should read prospectuses carefully.

Entry requirements depend on the individual course.

City and Guilds Professional Photographic Certificate 744 is for people already employed in photography or with promise of employment. Entrants need a minimum of two GCSEs or equivalent, including English.

BTEC/SCOTVEC National Certificate or Diploma courses require four GCSEs at grades A-C, or their equivalent, after which students may go on to study for the Higher National Certificate.

BTEC/SCOTVEC Higher National Diploma requires two A levels or equivalent.

These are two-year courses.

Vocational courses recognised by the British Institute of Professional Photographers (BIPP) require a minimum of four GCSEs or equivalent, and involve two years' full-time or three years' part-time study at a college of further education or one of a few polytechnics.

The BIPP Professional Qualifying Examination requires two A levels or equivalent, involving three years' full-time or the equivalent part-time study.

Degree courses in photography require at least two A levels or equivalent; or five GCSEs (or four plus an A level) or equivalent and a successfully completed one-year art and design foundation course.

FASHION MODELLING

Only a handful of people who dream of being a top model ever make it. It's not a question of being 'beautiful' – more important is to be photogenic and have the 'look' that is currently in demand. Some people stick to catalogue work, which demands a different look from magazines, advertising or the catwalk. Others specialise in just one of these areas – catwalks, for instance, involve a performance and are great for extroverts who enjoy applause! Almost all models are booked through agencies who have bookers to form the link between model and client.

MODEL

Sharron Fisher is a top international **model** who has worked for four years in magazine and advertising work:

'When I didn't get the A levels I wanted, someone suggested I become a model. I knew that Select was a reputable agency, handling top models so, with a little Dutch courage, I went and saw them. They immediately told me to lose two stones! They kept in touch over the next few months and then sent me to see photographers and magazines to get my face known. If they like the look of you, they take the photographs and you pay for what you want printed. Never pay in advance to have shots taken. Good agencies never charge for training. The agency will guide you through it all – they need to, because it's full of potential pitfalls.'

You have to be very careful when you're choosing the agency. Some are distinctly disreputable. Many of the reliable ones belong to the Association of Model Agents (AMA), which was formed specifically to protect the interests of agents and models. Agencies have to have been in business for at least two years before they are eligible. Beware of companies that advertise for models in magazines – these may look convincing but won't lead to a guarantee of work and may cost you a lot of money.

You will have to be prepared to pay for test shots, index cards and a portfolio case – but not before you've been accepted by a reputable agency. You will also have to be prepared to finance yourself for the first few months, since it's quite likely that you won't get much work initially. If you're successful though, the rewards are great ... but at a price:

'It can be hard work at times and very tedious, being treated like an object, with everyone staring at you. It's very strange and stressful in front of a camera at first – and the catwalk is an experience I prefer not to repeat! It's so frenzied. Some people love that thrill, the excitement – I found it terrifying! You have to feel confident to do this job well, so you choose the area of work that suits you best.

Sharron Fisher

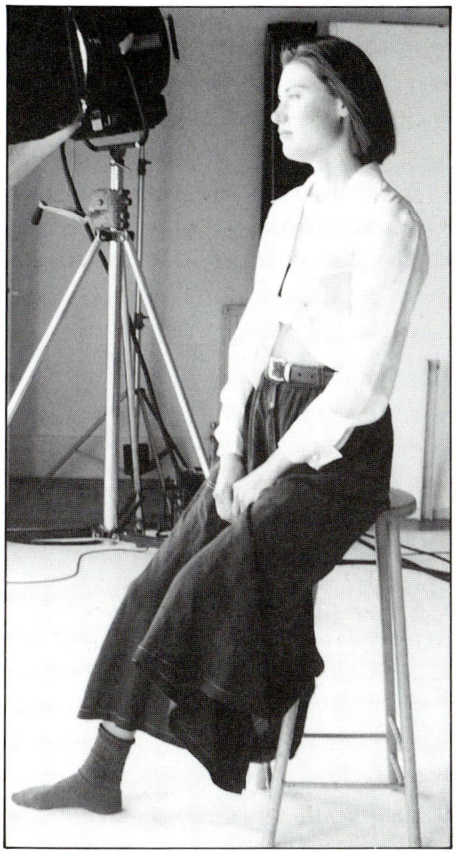

'I've travelled all over the world – America, Japan and throughout Europe (particularly Milan and Paris, where the collections are). A trip may last for a week or just a day; you may be busy for weeks and weeks and then have no work for a while. I didn't make any money for the first couple of years, but I was ploughing plenty in, working on editorial shoots and building up my portfolio.

'Now I concentrate on editorial and advertising work. It's not something I see myself doing forever. There's a high boredom factor, sitting around for hours after hair and make-up have finished, just waiting to start.

'At times it's glamorous, but you must never let it go to your head and start playing the prima donna – you simply won't be offered work again. You have to be responsible, disciplined and self-motivated or you won't get anywhere. I like aspects of the work – the money, the travel and the constant variety of people. I don't like the way it makes you become very self-critical!'

WAYS IN

Different agencies specialise in different types of models. Laraine Ashton, for instance is well-known for commercial models, used to advertise products. Fashion usually requires a stronger look – agencies to try include Select, Synchro, Storm and Take Two. Contact the Association of Model Agents (AMA) for their list of members. Either phone direct or send two snaps, one showing your face and the other showing your body shape, with a covering letter giving your height, body measurements and age. There's no need to go to the expense of having photos specially taken. All established agents will be able to give you an idea of your potential – if several agencies turn you down, they are probably right!

There is very little formal training, although the agency will give you advice about general appearance. The AMA positively discourages potential models from taking a private modelling course, since they can be expensive and are no guarantee of future work. If, however, you are looking for catwalk modelling or would like to work in-house for a fashion manufacturer, you may find it helpful. Such models are often required to do other work for their employee when they're not modelling – such as reception work or looking after buyers. The London College of Fashion runs a one-year course which covers secretarial and business skills as well as showroom, catwalk and photographic modelling. Applicants need to be over 16 years old with a minimum of three GCSEs or their equivalent.

Models have to conform to height, weight and age restrictions. 5′8″/5′9″ (1.73m) and over for a girl, 6′ to 6′2″ (1.83m) for a man; size 10 or small 12 for a girl, 38 or 40 for a man. Most start between the ages of 18 and 22, although a few start younger. A model's career normally lasts for between five and ten years for a girl, slightly longer for a man.

WHERE TO FIND OUT MORE

First find your course.

Consult:

- *The Directory of First Degree and Diploma of Higher Education Courses* (CNAA);
- DOFE – *The Directory of Further Education* (Hobsons);
- DUKHE – *The Directory of UK Higher Education* (Hobsons);
- Design Courses in Britain (Design Council);
- *University Entrance – The Initial Guide* (Sheed and Ward).

Ask at your local college or public library for information about courses you can take in your area.

For information about BTEC and SCOTVEC courses, write direct to them.

If money is no problem, it is possible to study at a prestigious American college (Parsons School of Design or the Fashion Institute of Technology in New York or the Fashion Institute of Design and Merchandising in Los Angeles) or one of the European universities (see *Higher Education in the European Community*, published by the European Community in conjunction with Kogan Page).

All these institutions are fee paying.

Useful Reading:

- *Vogue Guide to a Career in Fashion by Anne Matthews;*
- *Getting Jobs in Fashion Design – Cassell.*